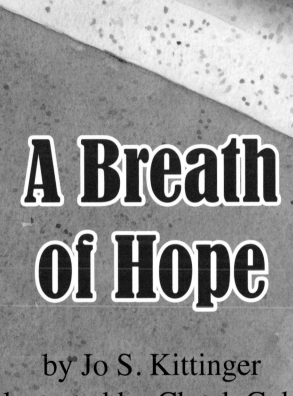

A Breath
of Hope

by Jo S. Kittinger
Illustrated by Chuck Galey

Dedication
The author wishes to acknowledge and thank Anthony H. Barash, a Harvard University Advanced Leadership
Initiative Fellow (2010), for his invaluable support of A Breath of Hope and for his innovative contributions to the
development of legal literacy as a tool of self-empowerment for those who are unable to afford legal assistance in
times of need.

Library of Congress Cataloging-in-Publication Data
Kittinger, Jo; 1955-
A Breath of Hope, Illustrator: Chuck Galey; 1954-
p.cm.

Summary; A young immigrant girl has a serious asthma attack due to mold in the family's landlord-neglected
apartment. Her brave brother helps her through the emergency and, through his interactions at the hospital, con-
nects his family with legal assistance to have the apartment refurbished.

[1. Asthma—Non-fiction. 2. Black mold—Non- fiction. 3. Immigrant's rights—Non-fiction. 4.Legal Assistance-
Non-fiction. 5. Medical-Legal Partnership-Non-fiction.]

A Breath
of Hope

by Jo S. Kittinger
Illustrated by Chuck Galey

I hold Isabel's hand and hum her favorite song.

It doesn't help. She gasps for each breath. Her lips are gray.

This is not Isabel's first asthma attack, but it *is* the first time

neither Mamá nor Papá are home. My teacher said to call 911

in an emergency, but Papá said ambulances cost too much

unless someone is dying.

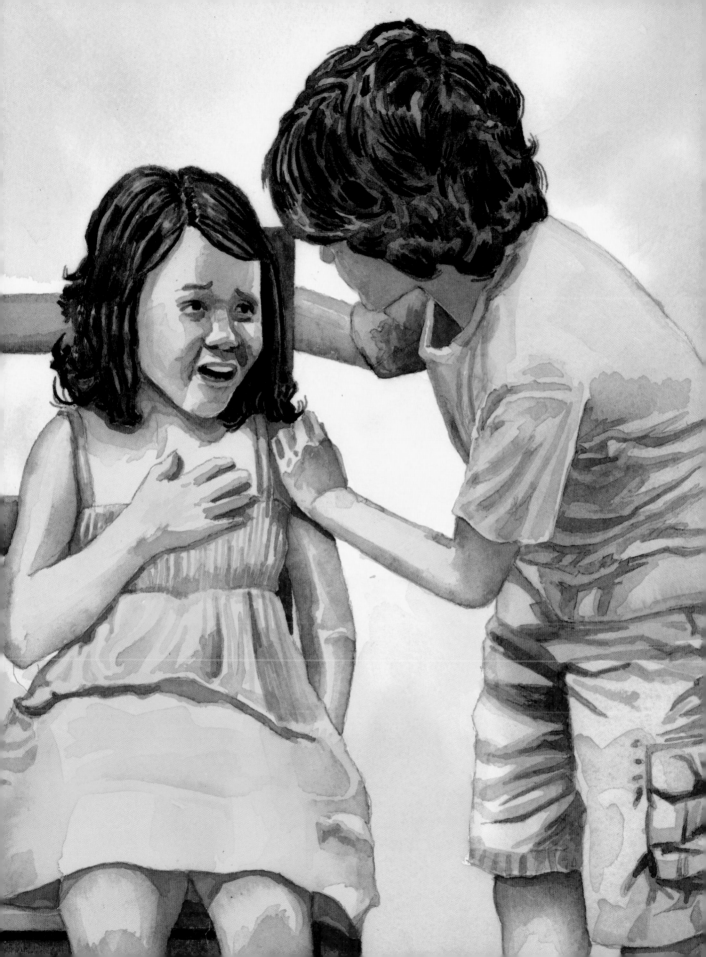

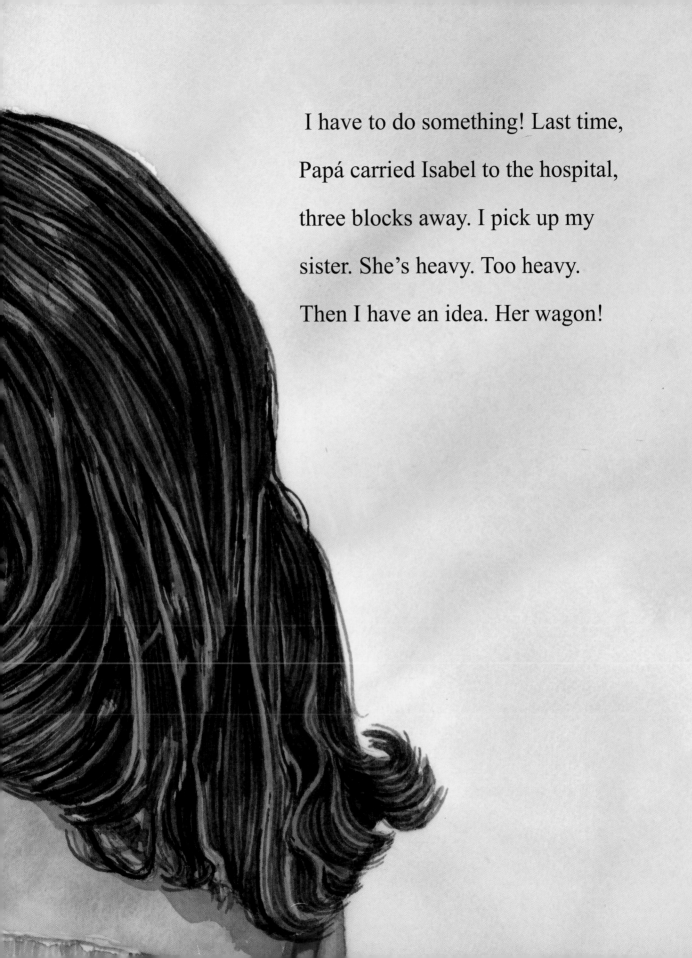

I have to do something! Last time,
Papá carried Isabel to the hospital,
three blocks away. I pick up my
sister. She's heavy. Too heavy.
Then I have an idea. Her wagon!

I set Isabel in the wagon and

pull it down the sidewalk.

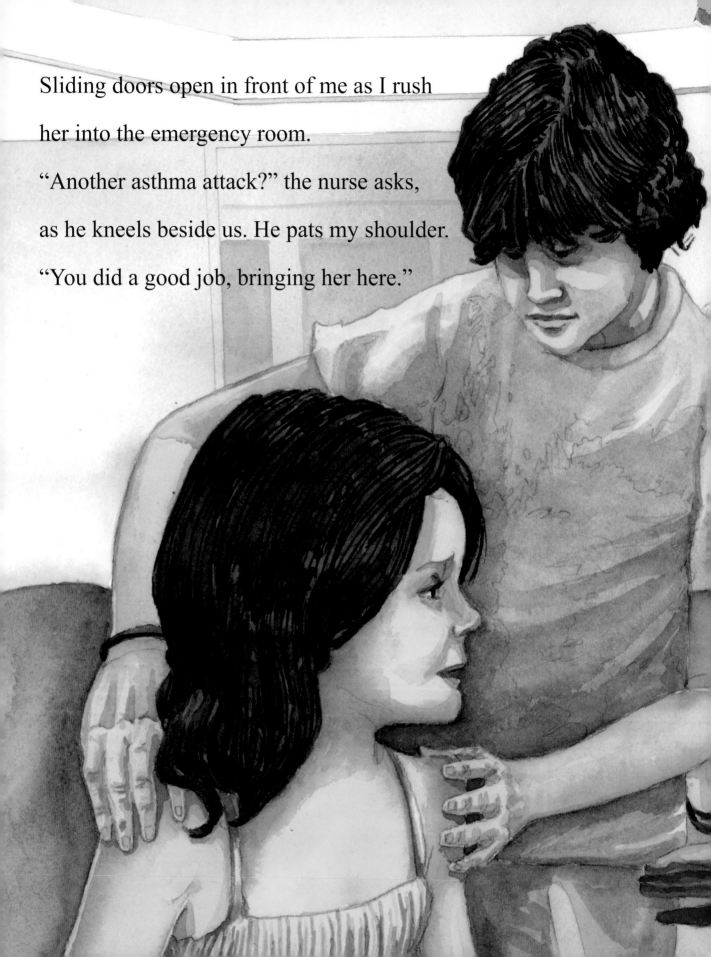

Sliding doors open in front of me as I rush

her into the emergency room.

"Another asthma attack?" the nurse asks,

as he kneels beside us. He pats my shoulder.

"You did a good job, bringing her here."

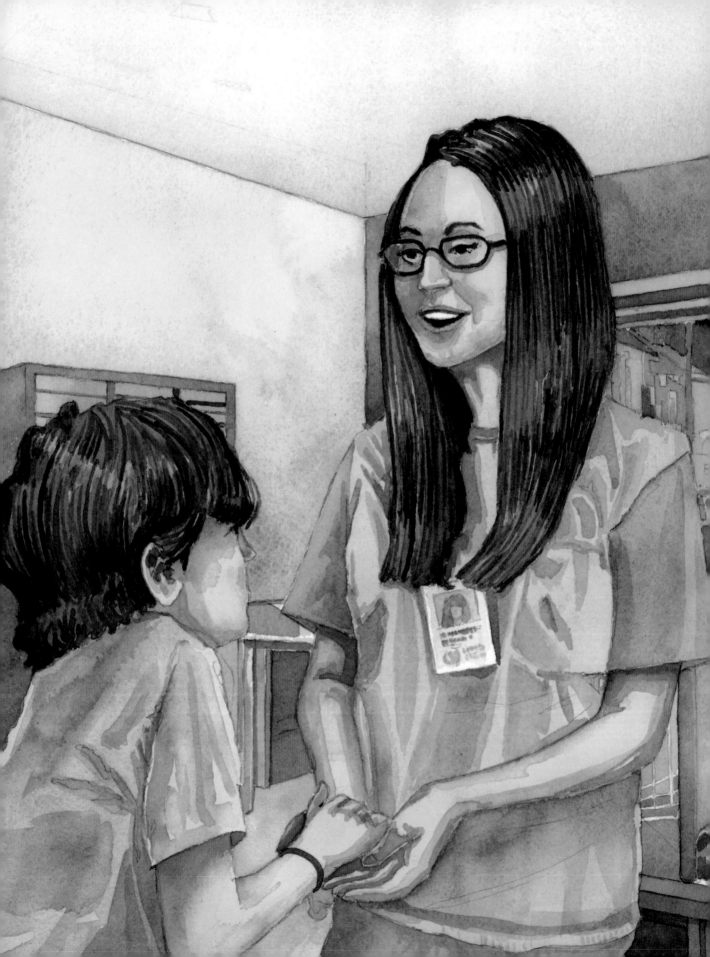

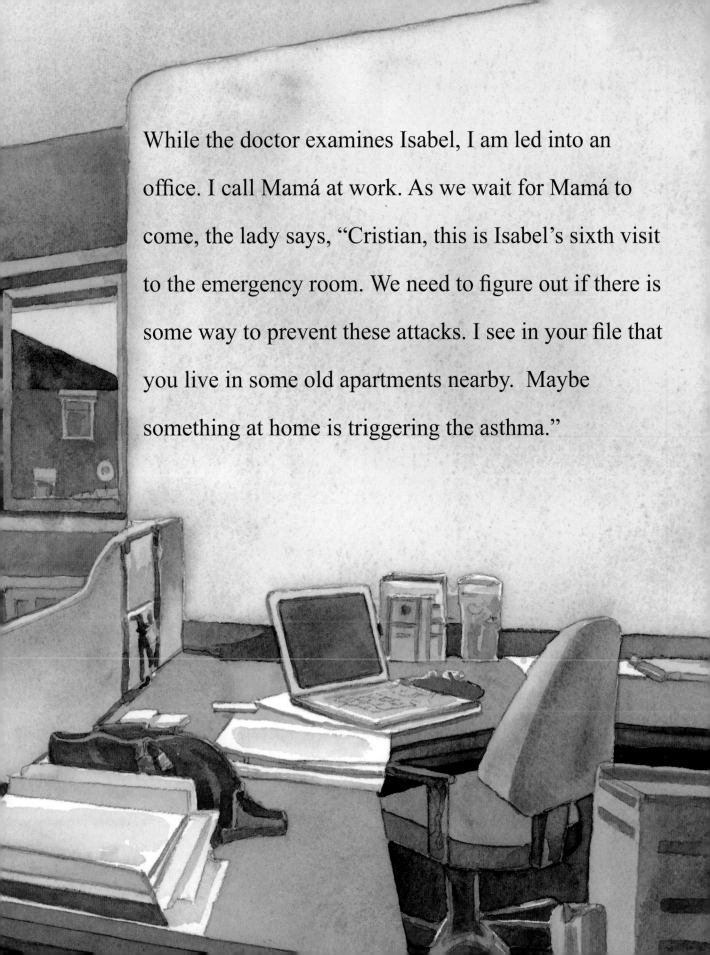

While the doctor examines Isabel, I am led into an office. I call Mamá at work. As we wait for Mamá to come, the lady says, "Cristian, this is Isabel's sixth visit to the emergency room. We need to figure out if there is some way to prevent these attacks. I see in your file that you live in some old apartments nearby. Maybe something at home is triggering the asthma."

"You're an important part of Isabel's medical team," the lady says. Then she asks me a million questions about our apartment.

Do we have dogs or cats?

Are there rats or mice?

Pigeons on the fire escape?

What do our ceilings and floors look like?

Are the walls wet or moldy?

"What's mold?" I ask.

"It looks like black dust growing on the walls or in the carpet," the lady says.

"Yes, mold," I say. "Lots of it. Mamá asked the landlord to fix our apartment. But he said our rent would go up if he does any work."

The lady takes my hand and we walk down the hall. "There is someone I want you to talk with," she says. "Ms. Bowman is a Medical-Legal Partner at the hospital. Perhaps she can help."

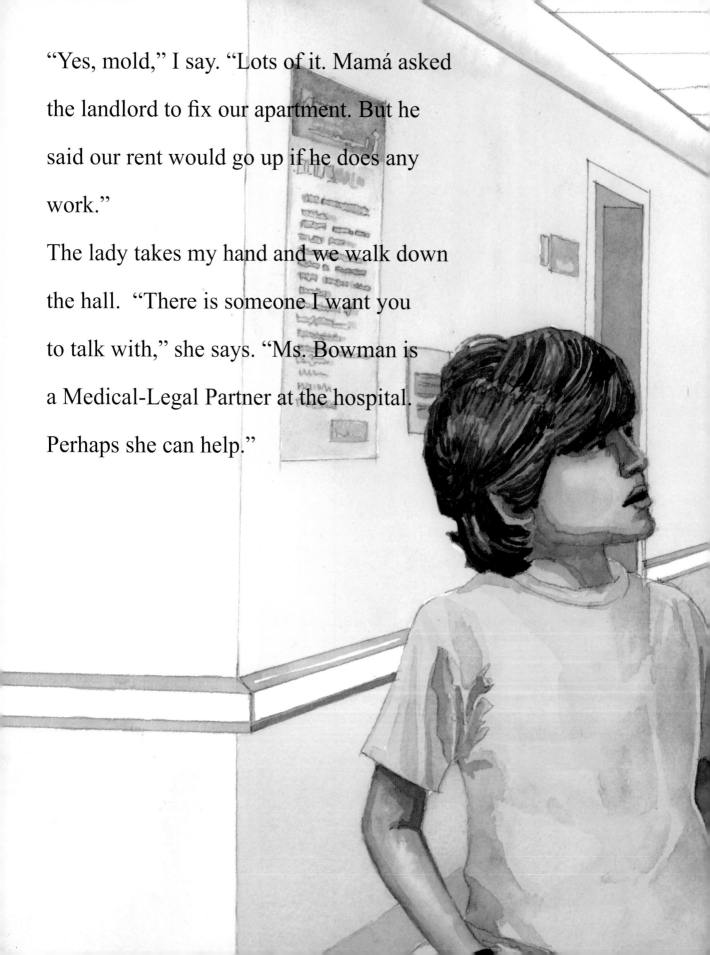

Mamá gets to Ms. Bowman's office at the same time. Isabel is with her! I'm so happy to see her breathing easy again.

Mamá talks and I translate. She's worried about how much money the hospital will want if Ms. Bowman helps.

"I work pro bono," Ms. Bowman says.

The look on my face tells her I don't understand.

"I volunteer my time," she says. "It's free." Mamá smiles when I translate.

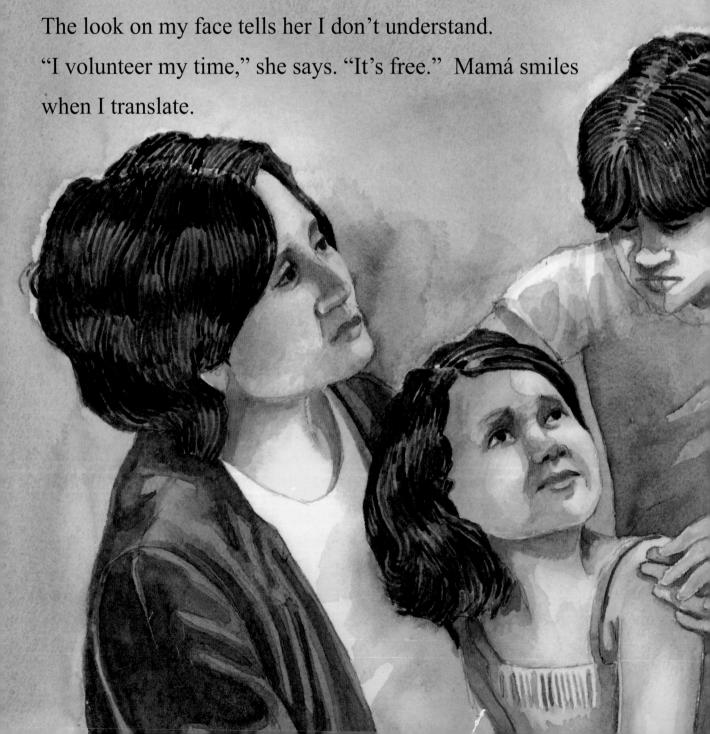

Ms. Bowman drives us back to our apartment and comes inside. She shakes her head and points out water leaks and mold in the carpet. Mamá says she's embarrassed, but Ms. Bowman says it is the landlord's fault. He should fix our apartment.

When Ms. Bowman explains that mold is
causing Isabel to be sick, Mamá starts to
cry.
She's afraid of the landlord,
afraid of being kicked out of the
apartment, and very afraid for Isabel.
"What can we do?" I ask.

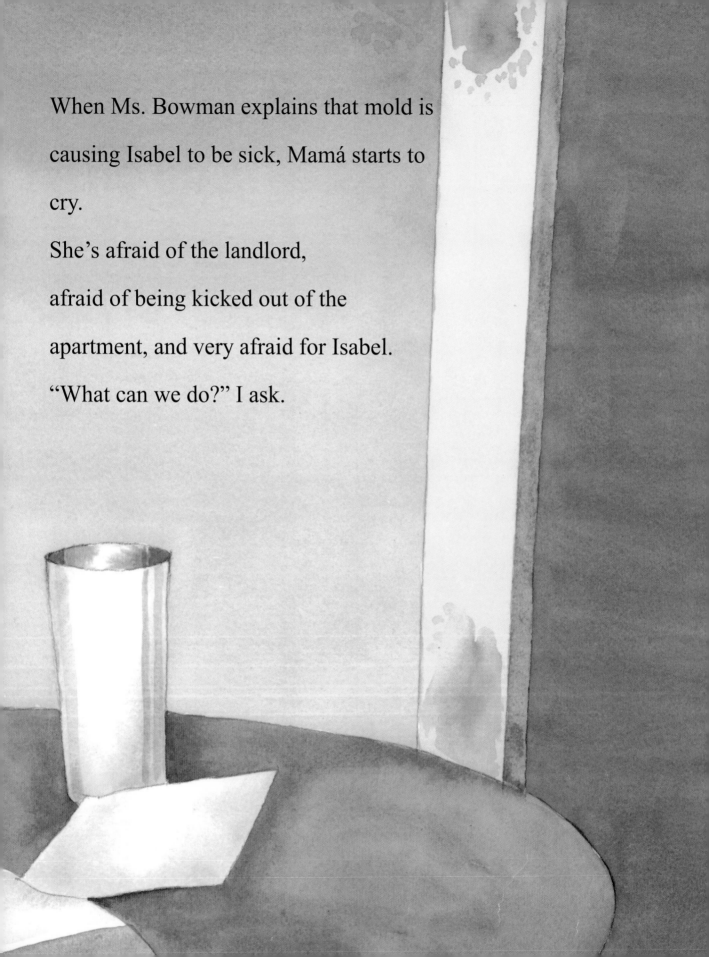

When Papá hears about the mold, he slams his fist on the table.

"That landlord is making my Isabel sick!"

"Papá, Ms. Bowman says we can fight with the law," I say and

hand Papa a brochure she gave me.

Two days later we get a serious-looking envelope in the mail from a lawyer's office. Mamá is afraid to open it. I tear into the letter and smile as I read. "It's a copy of the letter Ms. Bowman is sending to the landlord," I tell Mamá. "It says he must make repairs to our apartment and if he tries to raise the rent there will be trouble for him."

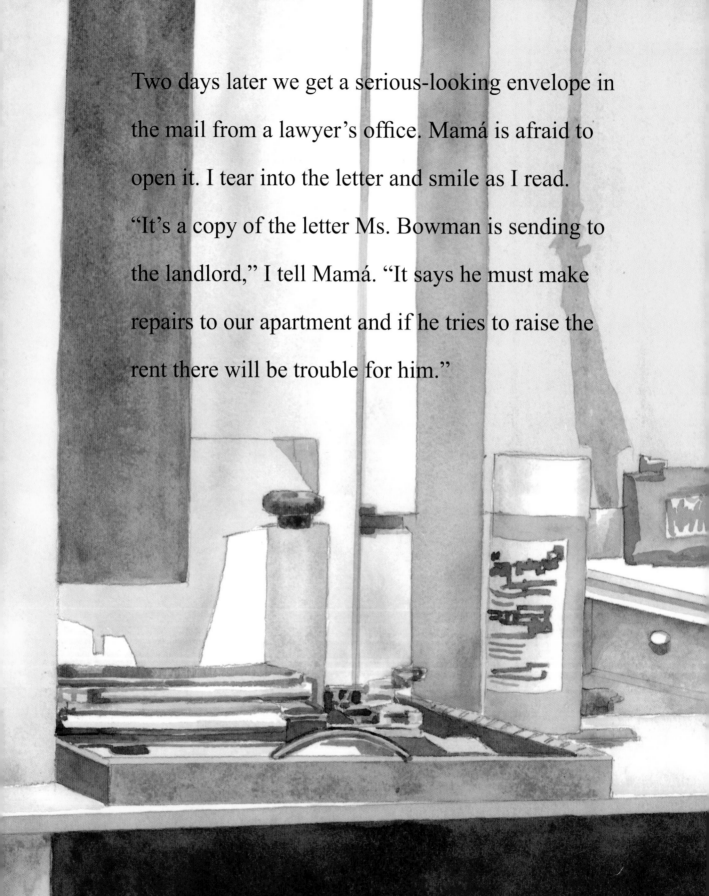

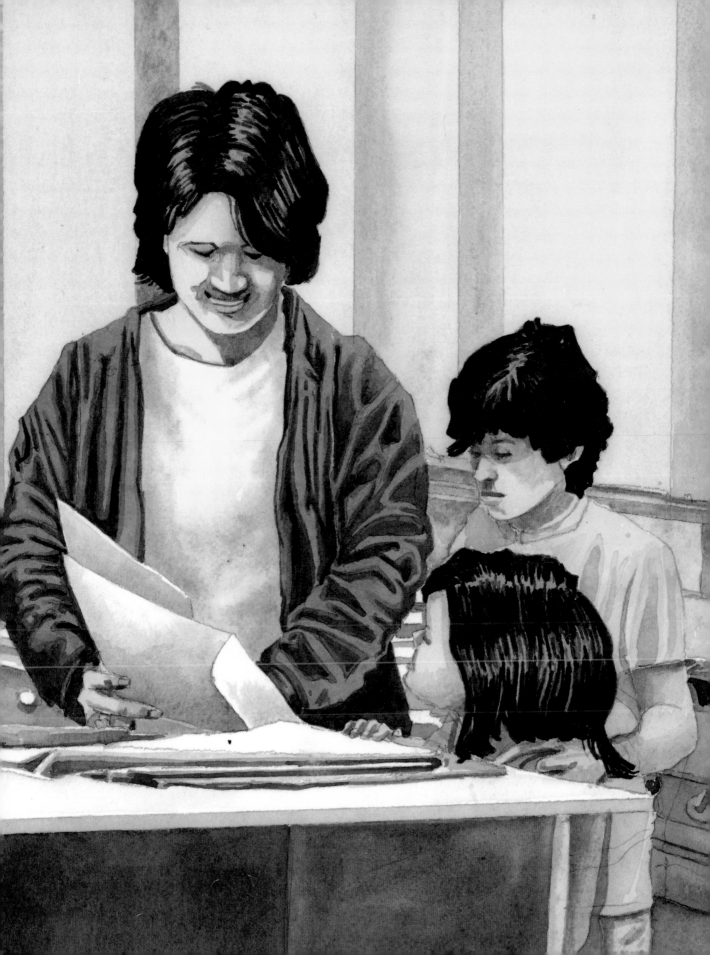

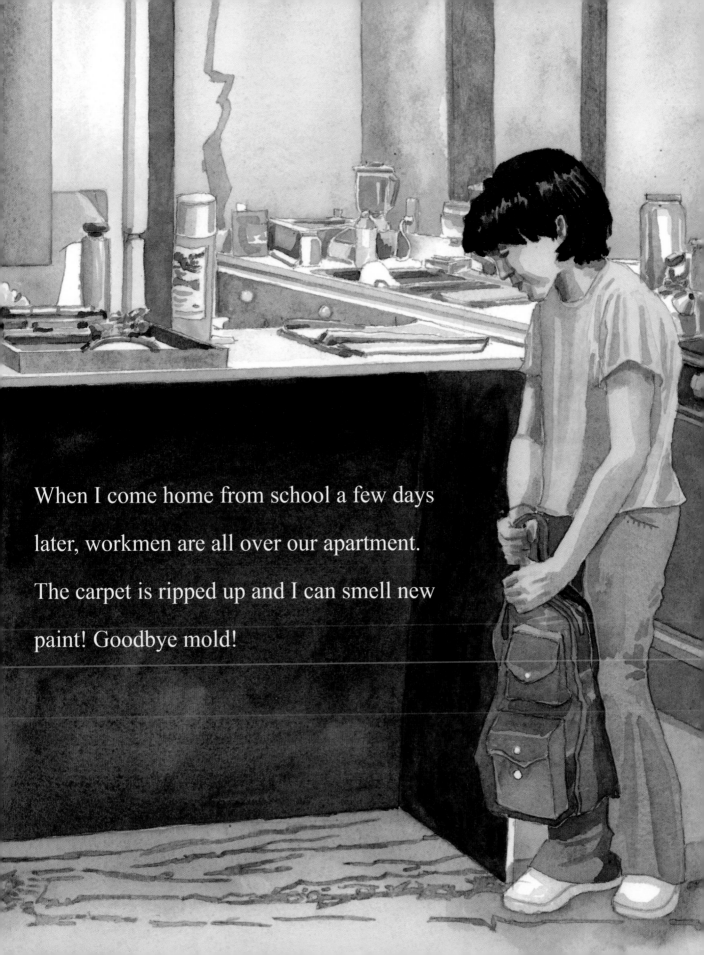

When I come home from school a few days later, workmen are all over our apartment. The carpet is ripped up and I can smell new paint! Goodbye mold!

And God bless Ms. Bowman.

Things You Should Know

Renter's Rights

If your family rents your apartment or home, you should know that most states have laws that require landlords to maintain apartments and houses with basic requirements such as: water, electricity, heat, weatherproofing, and sanitary, safe conditions.

Remember that your family can get help from lawyers, and if your family cannot afford a lawyer, the local bar association or legal aid organization in your community or neighborhood can refer you to a lawyer who assists you without expecting to be paid a fee.

Always write letters, keep copies, and take notes to show that you have made efforts to have the landlord repair your home. Keep those papers all together in a safe place. Your family, as a tenant, is responsible to keep your living space well-maintained and abide by the rules of your lease. If you are unsure regarding your housing rights, contact your local legal aid organization.

Medical-Legal Partnerships ("MLPs")

MLPs unite lawyers who provide free legal services at hospitals and health clinics with doctors to help patients and their families solve legal problems that cause or contribute to poor health. Often conditions such as unsafe housing can make it hard for a patient to get well. Other issues an MLP might help with include: housing, access to utilities, immigration, education, public benefits, guardianship, wills and family law.

For more information, go to the American Bar Association's Medical-Legal Partnership Pro Bono Support Project website at www.medlegalprobono.org or the National Center for Medical-Legal Partnership website at www.medical-legalpartnership.org

Legal Aid

Legal Aid organizations are located in many cities. They offer free or low-cost legal services to people who cannot afford to pay a lawyer. Often, there are special programs available for children, senior citizens or people with disabilities. These services can help with issues between tenants and landlords, including eviction, foreclosure, and substandard housing. A directory of legal aid organizations can be found at www.findlegalhelp.org .